Littoral

Also by Patricia Debney

How to Be a Dragonfly
Losing You

Patricia Debney

Littoral

for Mom —

Enjoy!

With all my love,

xxo P.

Shearsman Books

First published in the United Kingdom in 2013 by
Shearsman Books
50 Westons Hill Drive
Emersons Green
BRISTOL
BS16 7DF

Shearsman Books Ltd Registered Office
30–31 St. James Place, Mangotsfield, Bristol BS16 9JB
(this address not for correspondence)

www.shearsman.com

ISBN 978-1-84861-293-8

Acknowledgements
Littoral was written during a six-week residency in the Little Blue Hut on
the North Kent coast. I am grateful to Canterbury City Council for its
unconditional support.

'Half-Shell' previously appeared in *Did I Tell You? 131 Poems in Aid of
Children in Need* (WordAid, November 2010). 'Onshore Wind', 'Cross
Wind', 'Breaking', 'Making Waves' and 'This Time Tomorrow' previously
appeared in *slantways: an anthology of prose poems* (WordAid, March
2011). 'Littoral Drift', 'Rising Tide', 'Sea Breeze', 'Doldrums', 'Shadows',
and 'Becalmed at Half Tide' previously appeared in *Envoi* (Summer 2011).
'The Fetch', 'Little Blue Hut', 'Perfect Summer's Day 1' and 'Perfect
Summer's Day 2' previously appeared in *Shearsman* 91 & 92 (May 2012).

Accompanying definitions taken from the *Glossary of Coastal Definitions*,
Washington State Department of Ecology, http://www.ecy.wa.gov/
programs/sea/swces/products/glossary.htm, by permission of the
Washington State Department of Ecology.

Contents

iv.

AMPLITUDE: Half of the pea
of a WAVE. **AVULSION:** (1) E
by WAVES during a storm. (2
by flood, currents, or ch
water. **BASIN:** A large subma
circular, elliptical or ova
has become so steep that t
forward, moving faster tha
Breakers may be roughly
although there is much ove
and turbulent water spill
The upper 25 percent of the
before breaking. Breaking
distance. (2) Plunging - a
breaking is usually with a c
follows. (3) Collapsing - b
of WAVE. Minimal air pock
Bubbles and foam present. (
bottom rushes forward from
up BEACH FACE with little c
surface remains almost pl
be produced on the BEACH F
DEPTH: The still-water D
WAVE breaks. **CALM:** The co
when there is no WIND WAVE
A WAVE whose velocity o

o-trough range (or height)

EROSION of the shoreland

sudden cutting off of land

in course of a body of

DEPRESSION of a generally

hape. **BREAKER:** A WAVE that

crest of the WAVE topples

he main body of the WAVE.

ssified into four kinds,

p: (1) Spilling - bubbles

n the front face of WAVE.

nt face may become vertical

erally across over quite a

est curls over air pocket;

h. Smooth splash-up usually

king occurs over lower half

and usually no splash-up.

urging - WAVE peaks up, but

der WAVE, and WAVE slides

o bubble production. Water

except where RIPPLES may

during BACKWASH. **BREAKING**

at the point where the

tion of the water surface

r SWELL. **CAPILLARY WAVE:**

propagation is controlled

Littoral

i.

Littoral

Maybe you don't want to look. There, where the sand begins. From the eddies around, it could be a door. Part of a boat, or a warped bit of board someone used to walk on.

Anyway you don't get there quick enough. You watch as it goes under, each swell layering more water—first the navy blue blends, then the edges flare into sand.

It might be there next time, might not. It might be shunted somewhere—closer in, further out, then along some—and left to settle. Work its way into another version of this landscape.

Onshore Wind

In your own back garden, the sun bakes. New leaves unfold as you watch and tulips flood with high colour. The earth greens.

Here the seasons have different signals, and the tides repeat their complex but regular patterns regardless of temperature: diurnal, neap, equatorial, perigean. Algae bloom and fade, and barnacles cling and release, wash up in all weathers.

This is not about you. Or you. Or anything we might think responds to sun or shower, heat or cold, tenderness or neglect.

This blows a wind past you that was going to blow anyway. This sweeps sediment according to size and weight and deposits it further down the shore. This shapes whatever you do and have done.

You thought you had got to grips with the turning and tilting, and your place in it. The vegetable pattern of growth and death, the length of the arcs of parts of this life.

But here there is more grey. And no beginning, no end.

Whitstable Spit

It starts with the usual line of ripples, small crests. Some kind of meeting of the same but different, sixty degrees of separation.

The tide is coming in. The wind picks up. Rough and smooth battle over the high ground, white foam twisting and roiling all along the edge like the tail of a Chinese dragon, mobile as paper.

The sign warns of it. And now, after all this, the pebbled peninsula we stood on moments ago disappears. Horns locked, the sea closes in.

In truth it was never dependable. So the first thing to do is stop crying. Chances are you'll learn to walk along it when you can, and leave before you drown.

Shadows

If I knew how far away they were, and the angle of their advancing, I could work out the speed of the wind.

All morning they've come in rows, from first glance to hut to scarp in seconds, black ink trick, oil slick, dark army approaching.

Fear too comes and goes. Froth rolls grey and dirty up the shore.

While between times the bright sun turns it back to white. Like the clouds themselves when I can bring myself to look, watch them sail across clear blue sky.

Cross Wind

On the other side of the spit, water rages, shoulders some submerged punching bag that never gives an inch.

While over here, the tide curls its lips, laps against the shore, stretches, as if resting.

This morning the wind has swung right around. Which makes a nice change, I admit.

Sea Breeze

Out at sea, the water browns with it. Waves scud along for meters, in a race where no one knows the beginning or end. For miles they break through, foaming, like underwater creatures coming up for air.

I expected wind. But not like this. Some days it pushes me back from the shore. Muscles in around these window frames, up the sleeves of this heavy coat. Some days it literally takes my breath away.

Doldrums

Late afternoon. A cross wind, or offshore. Or onshore, depending. The water shifts minute by minute, and for the first time the turbines hardly turn.

The breeze blows down my neck like a message. Something to remember, or forget. To long for, or reject. Regret. Resist or give in to. Too many useless things to do.

The sun warms one side. White clouds thin. And the tide slinks down the beach, water greying, brown algae emerging, gulls fly in.

All this was bound to happen. You signed on for the duration. Wait now to be moved.

primarily by the surface ter
WAVE is travelling. A water
is less than 2.5 cm is cons
See also RIPPLE. **COASTLIN**
that forms the boundary bet
(2) Commonly, the line tha
land and the water. **CRO**
state of the SEA due to d
different directions raise
OF CURRENT: Direction tow
DIRECTION OF WAVES: Dir
coming. **DIRECTION OF WIN**
is blowing. **EBB:** Period whe
taken to mean the EBB CUR
period. **EROSION:** Wearing
forces. On a BEACH, the car
WAVE action, TIDAL CURRENTS
A more or less continuous
facing in one general di
EROSION or faulting, also c
of unobstructed OPEN SEA
can generate WAVES (GENERAT
a strong breeze and a sto
in degrees of moderate, fr
varying in velocity from
hour. **GENERATING AREA:** In

n of the liquid in which the

E in which the WAVE LENGTH

ed to be a capillary wave.

(1) Technically, the line

n the COAST and the SHORE.

orms the boundary between

SEA: Confused, irregular

rent groups of WAVES from

y local winds. **DIRECTION**

which CURRENT is flowing.

ion from which WAVES are

Direction from which wind

IDE level is falling; often

which occurs during this

y of the land by natural

g away of BEACH material by

by DEFLATION. **ESCARPMENT:**

of CLIFFS or steep SLOPES

tion which are caused by

d SCARP. **FETCH:** The length

ace across which the wind

AREA). **GALE:** A wind between

A continuous wind blowing

strong, or whole gale and

to 30 NAUTICAL MILES per

E forecasting, a continuous

ii.

Tsunami

The sun shines. The parade fills with solo runners, then empties, fills again with couples and dogs and bikes and mothers with prams and children. They settle on the beach.

I remember: those minutes elongated into endless present, the halting walk down the shingle, constant undertow of fatigue. The pull on our sleeves to remark upon this stone, that gull on the post, a ship at sea, our son's hand poised like a visor, like a sailor he might have seen on tv.

It comes at me straight, no escape: this is how it used to be. No tracking shifting shorelines, no distance crest to crest. No seismograph, no breaking news, no scouting for tremors.

At the moment of change we long for whatever leaves us. We stumble, stripped, all landmarks razed.

Breaking

There is elegance in public drama. You curl, arch over like a dancer, plunge. The foam is clean white, short-lived, and dies, swooning, right at the feet of the shore.

Or tell no one. Reach the point where your legs buckle, pull out from under. Collapse. We've all done it. Only a few bubbles on the surface to show for it. When you can touch bottom again, stand up.

Or this morning. The long, slow spill. Posts shake in their moorings, flags whip back, and there is nothing you can do but feel it come in waves that topple way out to sea, and are dragged, still raging, head under, for meters more than you thought possible.

This only happens rarely, and requires certain conditions. A fast-rising tide, deceptive incline, relentless wind.

Rising Tide

There is a point when water comes in more quickly. You can say it's the relative depths of nearshore and foreshore. You can recall how the gulls are able to stand a long way out, how the incline isn't steep.

Only it always surprises me. Comes in at a rush. A white marker I put up is swallowed. A patch of stones clings on in the backwash. And I find I'm moving my shoes above the flood mark. Again.

Gravity Waves

The wind sets them up. Somewhere out of sight, beyond the turbines and the distant North Sea vessels on the horizon, something gets them started: a storm, a change in pressure, or maybe just the predictable cycle of seasonal gusts.

The earth keeps them going. In spite of herself, she can't let go. The relentless movement wearies, wears and sometimes she suffocates—but there's no stopping swells. Like children, they addle her surface.

Eventually they will die at sea, or break against some shore.

Sky & Sea

How can this water be so grim, raging brown and grey, while overhead there's pure violet, white fluffy, electric blue?

This may reveal my fundamental idealism. Because I picture our existence

> as the messy in-between, this complicated *air*, so fragile or deadly, so uncertain and open to chance —somewhere indeed   so chaotic that if it weren't for the irrefutable and ever harmonious, corresponding expanses of stratosphere, water and land—

> keeping it neat as a sandwich—

I could not bear to live here…

Or this may reveal my ignorance of the fundamentals of the physical sciences. Of which I am only sometimes and necessarily aware.

High Tide at the Spit

There must be a name for the moment of change. When confusion, however beautiful, leaves us, and regular, longshore waves fold themselves at our feet.

At last glance we were all frolics and swells, outright playful splashes. White foam skipping boundaries. Ripples widening like batter right to the edges of the pan.

Before that: glass stillness, whitetops, diamond makings and breakings, points of intersection delineating a straight line along underlying sand.

And in the beginning: two sides of a triangular bit of land, little peninsula sunk in jade green. How fast will the water come in? Are those fish? How long will this last?

Life tends toward the universal: wind and gravity and the changing shape of the shore mean waves travel the same direction eventually, at the same speed, in the same general fashion.

Whatever, you understand, may lie beneath.

Avulsion

A word that might have made its stealthy way into our everyday.
So rich on the tongue, taking up so much space: an acquired
taste perhaps like truffles, foie gras. Offal. Perhaps at first we spit
it out, eject it. Rejection.

Perhaps then a bird? Outside a ragged gull cries inconsolable, no
breath left. It flits along the shore in apparent desperation, low
and hoping someone—anyone—stops this spiralling flight.

Or what everyone avoids. Some stinking condition of the body.
An incurable infection or growth.

No. The stormy waves erode with such abandon that the land
you thought safe cuts off from shore. A few violent minutes seal
your fate.

You had no way of knowing, had never even heard it said.

Hindsight

So much comes down to physics. The angle of this, speed of that, trajectory of the other... Even all this irregular crashing—the highs and lows—of these fast waves can be drawn on a graph.

And why this groyne over that? Why the angling of the water here, the deep pulling back, the flat shore, the lines of froth out there... What invisible forces are at work?

Of course, there are equations for all this. Explanations. Diagrams. Whole exhaustively researched books.

But you don't think to ask.

Making Waves

It's true we can ride most things out. We track them approaching
and know we go up and over, brace ourselves for the drop. And
in clear water, we see them coming.

Only this is what happens: you rock the boat. You tip it from
side to side and front to back, and believe me it feels dangerous.

My sea legs fail. I curl my fingers round the rim, imagine mouth
to mouth. Battle through some freak storm.

Did you know one third of all waves are classed *significant*?
Enough of them and you or me—one of us—goes overboard.

The Fetch

This particular wind has blown a long way over open water. Dipping down like a bird or swirling up out of sight, but mostly held tight to the tops of numerous waves, at once urging and holding on for life.

A distance I've travelled. Between continents, across years. Land mass after land mass, hillock and cliff, shore and flowering wood—all could have stopped me. Should have, perhaps.

Today is frighteningly brisk. It wouldn't take much to tear a sail, collapse some stones. Let go the rope. I'm so tired, now that I think about it, of keeping us afloat.

Leeway

Right after it happened, there was no room for us. Our patch of land disappeared.

The wind whipped us, beat us on shingle.

        I drowned in sky, darkened sea, sand.

                Your face collapsed to stone.

***

We had to learn
About boats
Their leeward sides
Along the shore
Shelter
For every storm

Perfect Summer's Day 1

At a certain point, the sun and clear blue sky and turquoise sea wipe the slate clean. You notice instead the ways gulls chase, two on two, unsettling each other like relay runners, passing an invisible baton: *your turn now to fly low*, test good weather and calm water. Together you pass over, descend, move along the shore, your wings in unison, bare centimetres from a splash, crash and headlong fall.

Despite the dangers you hold onto your hard-won momentum, stay in the race.

Perfect Summer's Day 2

For a moment I'm thinking *anything is possible*. I can run and my knees won't give way. You could phone and sound the same. I won't burn in this sun, and everyone here is in love.

And to step on water is to step on land. To glide on one is to slide along the other. There is no shingle, no failure to reach the horizon, no treading water, no going under, no running to catch up, no giving in, no heartbreak and no letting go.

Perfect Summer's Day 3

Today I can admit this is harder than anything we have ever done or could imagine. In twenty years I have almost lost you—twice—and you've almost lost me too. Your mother, my grandparents, two pregnancies, and the silted accumulation of the forgotten or misplaced. All disappeared.

And now this: our first-born walks along a cliff, forever high over deep water. Nothing put him there, and nothing can save him.

I'm sorry makes no sense. But is true.

I say this now because the day can take it. Such calm water, and so much cloudless blue.

area of the water surface
essentially the same directi
with FETCH LENGTH. **GRADIE**
or water-surface) in meter
horizontal distance. **GRAVI**
of propagation is controll
WAVES more than 5 cm long
WAVES longer than 2.5 cm a
indeterminate zone betweer
See RIPPLE. **HEAVY SEA:**
high. **HINTERLAND:** The regi
HORIZON: The line or cir
boundary between Earth and
toward which the prevailing
toward which WAVES are tra
pertaining to, a SHORE, es
Living on, or occurring on,
The sedimentary material mo
the influence of WAVES and
SAND, or GRAVEL material m
in the NEARSHORE ZONE by W
Parallel and close to the
with periods above about 3
WAVE GROUPS breaking in th
portion of the TIDE that
attraction to the Moon. **N**

r which the wind blows in
Sometimes used synonymously

A measure of SLOPE (SOIL-
rise or fall per meter of

AVE: A WAVE whose velocity
rimarily by gravity. Water
considered gravity waves.
horter than 5 cm are in an
PILLARY and GRAVITY WAVES.
A in which the WAVES run
ying inland from the COAST.
which forms the apparent
y. **LEEWARD:** The direction
d is blowing; the direction
ing. **LITTORAL:** (1) Of, or
ally a SEASHORE. (2) (SMP)
SHORE. **LITTORAL DRIFT:** (1)
in the LITTORAL ZONE under
rrents. (2) (SMP) The mud,
parallel to the SHORELINE
and CURRENTS. **LONGSHORE:**
STLINE. **LONG WAVES:** WAVES
conds; can be generated by
RF ZONE. **LUNAR TIDE:** The
be attributed directly to
TIDE: TIDE of decreased

iii.

Cleaving

When the baby comes, there's an unexpected loss. Once joined now separated, once full now emptied. Once your body knows everything, then you know nothing.

The longer your child lives, the further from your body she grows: weans, washes, dresses, sleeps over. Takes notes in books you think you might read, but don't.

I'm trying to remember when we split. Can you? Nature says we were one big, one small. One feeder, one hungry. Once.

On the beach today I see another open shell, gaping like a purple mouth, or heavy wings. Easy to break them apart, but somehow they've lasted.

Unlike us. You at least would say the same. I wonder too if you would say you lost me right away, that the surgeon wielded the knife.

Nothing to do with you. Or me.

Celestial Mechanics

We start from water. Are occupied by its eddies and currents, sustenance and destruction.

Soon we contemplate waves, their distances, heights, and speeds. What makes them? What breaks them? How do they fashion the shore?

Only a few steps and we're on the long climb up the scarp. Here we trace the wind, the mud, the currents and gulls in our panoramic view.

And throughout, the tides. Relentless and almost magical at first, they creep and surge, change the landscape as we observe.

Twenty-five years after walking away from you, I examine the forces of nature, face your treasured equations. Newton was right: the moon perturbs the earth. The earth, the moon. And the sun, even at such a distance, perturbs them both.

We know this much, but not enough. No one can predict the subtleties of motion, the infinitesimal how and when. Which probably aggrieves you. For the same reasons it pleases me.

Florida, 1970–1982

Half a world away in length and width, and yet today unearths rare footage, muddies waters. Gulls as big as turkeys fight over what's been uncovered:

a wide sky
rotting fish
empty shells

Is this all you remember? The low capillary waves look uniform, stretch across the shore in military fashion. You wait for them to deepen and rush at last to dry land.

You watch for half an hour, for the suffocating advance. But at this time of day and in this terrain, no progress can be made. These silent waves sift forward just short of their falling back.

Near Atlantic City, 1976

A stroll across the dusty road and there's a beach, nearly empty, no shelter. Almost out of sight and closer to the city, boys pull their cars up to the shore, shouting at unpredictable intervals like sea birds.

Scrub and cigarette butts catch in my sandals. I walk toward the pine wood in the distance, away from all this.

Out of sight, the shore opens up, looping green pools and overhanging trees. There's a disused pier bleached grey, two planks, wide as my hips.

I strip, lie down on hot wood. The sun bakes, sand flakes along my skin, dries to a crust. Underneath, warm water churns and laps the shore and posts, aching with life. Above, white sky erases me.

This might be a dream. But I know the place exists.

Kiawah Island, 1980

For a time that summer we were friends on holiday. A swimming pool like I'd never seen, acres of green and miles of hard fine sand. You tried to teach me to play tennis on the beach, laughing in the stinging wind.

I didn't have the right clothes, or hat, or sunglasses. I had never tasted the wine or tropical fruits your parents offered me at mealtimes.

But I learned fast.

The night you told me you loved me, reached across the space between our beds for my hand, I ignored the quiet closing of some distant shell: *this again.*

Back in our mountain town, trees obscured the lay of the land. I couldn't tell you, and you couldn't ask. For the next three years you circled my house, your car horn sounding like a siren.

Whitetops

A nudge   a knock

                    attempt to smooth   near-stumble

        bright idea

uneven fringe

                controlled burp.

Lost words

        atonal moments

                blow after blow

                        to the head.

No Horizon

Is the sea in retreat, or pushing near? Beyond here, the sky could be a piece of paper, faint strata of yellowed tea stain, too long by the window in the sun.

Or a canvas. Rothko's final years: black on grey, brown, pressed grey on grey.

The edge is one third up, two-thirds down the pane. It continues out of sight, or is unseen. Touched, or never reached.

And here's the thing: his agonies, this endlessness of sky and sea, the impossibility of ordinary being.

Barely grey bleeds into chalk white that disappears. Yet remains. Brown becomes the sky. And black, that last rush across the page. Even this thin line, for him and all of us, fades. His red blood sprays and sprays, finally makes its mark.

Collected Shells

A few days later the hut smells.

Which goes to show I guess:

> ignorance is no defence
> and like he says
> this partly living
> is as good as dead.

Hinterland

What's there: four houses I remember, eight cats, one tree. Potted plants of different sizes, some living, some not. Dense mountains.

Rain. Snow. Heat.

Stone driveways. Wooden porches with cigarette butts underneath. Lost bracelets and socks, worn shoes, swollen windows and doors. Darkness. Silence. Empty streets.

A few friends. Some long-buried family.

Deep soil and rock. Digging in the same unyielding spot.

Slack Tide

We've all had them. Times of falling into stillness. Neither coming nor going. Waiting for evaporation.

The prospect brings relief. Quiet enough to disappear. Nothing of consequence anywhere.

Only: the moment does not exist. Of course, we know this. Sometimes we understand what's happening under the surface. And sometimes whatever happens, happens.

range occurring semimonthl

being in quadrature. **NEAF

an indefinite zone extendi

well beyond the BREAKER Z

terminology, the comparativ

extending from the SHOREFAC

SHELF. It is continually

seaward from the SHORE. **OF

seaward from the land in th

A wind blowing landward fro

For a plunging wave, the

over and breaks. (2) The

WAVES just before the water

(1) The light fretting or

the water caused by a bree

WAVES and one in which the

a significant degree, both

SIGNIFICANT WAVE: A stat

one-third highest WAVES of

by the average of their hei

(SLACK TIDE): The state

velocity is near zero, e

reversing current changes

is zero. The term is also

of low velocity near the t

when it is too weak to be

s the result of the moon

RE: In beach terminology
seaward from the SHORELINE
 OFFSHORE: (1) In beach
flat zone of variable width,
the edge of the CONTINENTAL
merged. (2) The direction
ORE WIND: A wind blowing
astal area. **ONSHORE WIND:**
he SEA. **PLUNGE POINT:** (1)
t at which the WAVE curls
al breaking point of the
shes up the BEACH. **RIPPLE:**
ffling on the surface of
(2) The smallest class of
rce of restoration is, to
rface tension and gravity.
ical term relating to the
ven WAVE GROUP and defined
 and periods. **SLACK WATER**
a TIDAL CURRENT when its
cially the moment when a
direction and its velocity
lied to the entire period
of turning of the current
any practical importance

iv.

Little Blue Hut

Another clear morning in high wind. At home you've left cats warming and rolling on the drive, the lime green of new-leaved trees, fragile pink of apple blooms.

Overhead now, a dozen gulls circle, riding something, searching, saying something or nothing. White as clouds in the cloudless sky, they somehow lead you.

Here you have come to expect the unexpected. To abandon plans. Look elsewhere for dependable weather.

Day after day the wind blows in. And you press further and further out from your wooden house, tip seaward with no rudder and no soil to hold you. Only air speeds, tides and currents, temperatures and moisture to go by. The mysterious, unfixed sky, these shifting waters, endless hidden gradients of land.

Becalmed at Half Tide

From the top of the scarp, the North Sea rolls out below like raw silk, embroidery along the shore, ruffled skirts of a stingray at rest.

This morning every catastrophe is elsewhere. And long ago, in deep water: storms, shipwrecks, miles of swells.

Here only the edges ripple. The sky and sea shine pearly as the insides of shells, in opalescent steel blue drifts, pink-white light where the sun breaks through.

There's no sign of a horizon. And no need to get there, or come back.

Clear Air

The wind farm has crept closer. In a private game of Grandma's Footsteps, I've caught the turbines mid-run, clownish soldiers, propellers waving awkward feathers on their heads.

They might be old hands at this:

> minute shuffle forward

> innocent spring back

> some silent dance

> quantum physics advance

> surpassing time and tides.

Or maybe in a gust of wind they just sense a gap and go, find themselves here and now, fresh-faced outside my window.

In Offshore Wind

Incoming

A warm land breeze ruffles the sea.

              Smooth fabric rises
                                stands
                                inverts
             shadows float
      to deeper waters.

Today is an illusion: wind upends the waves, polishes them like stone.
Devious water eats the shore.

***

Ebb

At the appointed hour, waves start again in the distance, like
music rolling near. They ripple

       sections   in   graphic   score
            staggered   some
     notes   sustained
          others   fading   out.

A desperate performance: earth and moon always outplay wind.
The waves make land though, hold tight enough, strike up a
furious band.

Tankerton Slopes

From here one end of the curve is the metropolis of Herne Bay—
at the other, the EAT HERE weather-beaten boards of Whitstable
seafront.

Between these two points then I am suspended, the curve of the
shore like the outer edge of a bowl, green rimmed, cooling in a
conservatory, light breeze passing through.

I might dip in, swim. Or keep walking all the way to Ramsgate.
Or take flight, my borrowed windproof puffed out in perfect
wings.

Each day is a gift. The wind blows.

Half Shell

A curled piece of butter. One petal. Tiny sea-horse mouth poking out.

Worked dough of a soft roll you might be making, or a fancy biscuit. The shape of your grown-up thumb along one side, where you might press.

The insides of things. The beautiful-what's-left. The palest coral blush. What you might have slipped in your pocket at nursery: torn off wool, acorn hat, worn stick.

The part of you that protects. And is protected.

What to Wear

The sea is the silver back of a mirror this morning, nearly white in the heat and sun, deepening here to pewter blue.

This morning the water, the distance and half circle of this bay make the dressing table I've never had. The uneven mirror, pieces of fabric to gauge: brushed silk, rubbed velvet, grosgrain.

I have all the time I need to brush my hair. The air will only get warm. The wind will remain a light breeze. And if I stare and stare, I will see the surface shifting, blinking, re-arranging, gradual movements, overall agreements and fallings into place, who I am and will be.

There's no hurry. The aim is clarity. Soon my whole reflection will be sky.

Neap Tide

It reeks of melancholy: one step forward, two steps back. Past the last post, the abandoned cupboard door, the tyre in better times a bath or trap for food: now the same pattern of green algae.

Meanwhile here the slow trickle continues, the left-behind pockets finally worked free and rushing down the beach. Sea gulls stand around and bicker over scraps.

Waves continue to crest at sea. The most able among us walk all the way down to the beach, the water's edge. The rest—poised with towels, stones to throw, dogs and sticks to find—stay up by the path, wait for time to pass, hands on our hips or shading our eyes.

Almost Gone

Outside the wind changed direction while I was sleeping. It blows me in gusts offshore, away from all this.

My red suitcase and purple hat wait by the door. Who'd have thought that waves turn back? That their energy reverses, flips over, reflecting the mottled shoreline, with its shingle and rock and occasional smooth sand, out into open water?

Some days you work against the tides, some days the winds. Or they intersect, strata shifting in infinite variations, patterns and straight lines, ruffles or hard edges depending on how you and they turn.

Little did I know how much I might leave onshore, or how much I might carry. And what returns to the sea.

This Time Tomorrow

Half an hour from this time tomorrow, you will go out onto the spit again. You will take each step as the water peels back.

You'll wade in, then watch your feet dry as the tide recedes. Move as far as you dare into the low waves rolling up the bank, see the light crystallise the eddies to almost solid, then watch them disappear.

You will find that the way opens out to you. That you will not be cut off and left for dead, your children crying for their mother, your husband scanning the horizon forevermore.

In so many ways, it's that simple. The more you walk here the more you know the tides, the play of wind and gravity, and land. The easier it is to stand.

in navigation. The relation
the tidal phases varies in
places slack water occurs
water, while in other local
midway between HIGH and LC
accumulation of SAND or SH
with the COAST, with one
other projecting into the
ESTUARY. **SWELL:** WAVES that
from their GENERATING AREA
travel into LONG WAVES of
TIDE: The periodic rising
results from gravitationa
sun acting upon the rotat
high-velocity wave generat
floor (such as sudden faul
activity); also called se
oscillatory movement in a
alternate rise and fall of
of the surface of a liqui
form of a ridge, SWELL o
froth on CRESTS of WAVES
blowing the crest forward
material mark placed at a
from a property corner, an
station, as an aid in its

the time of slack water to
ferent localities. In some
 the times of high and low
s the slack water may occur
ATER. **SPIT:** A long narrow
E, lying generally in line
 attached to the land the
 or across the mouth of an
ve traveled a long distance
d have been sorted out by
 same approximate period.
 falling of the water that
traction of the moon and
earth. **TSUNAMI:** A large,
y displacement of the sea
, landsliding, or volcanic
c sea wave. **WAVE:** (1) An
 of water manifested by an
 surface. (2) A disturbance
ody, as the OCEAN, in the
ump. **WHITECAP:** The white
 wind (caused by the wind
 over). **WITNESS MARK:** A
wn distance and direction
trument station or a survey
covery and identification.

Lightning Source UK Ltd.
Milton Keynes UK
UKOW050521110713

213564UK00001B/12/P

9 781848 612938